Praise for *Carniva*

"*Carnival Mirror's* depth lies in its simplicity. It is a story of perseverance, personal evaluation, and triumph. A read that is captivating and practical. It gives you the ability to reflect on your own life and see the tides of your own self esteem, whether they be low or high. *Carnival Mirror* gives you sound and simple steps to strengthening your own self esteem."

—Leah Vanpoelvoorde, Synergy Work, Inc, Life/Business Coach

"*Carnival Mirror* is like reading someone's diary, their innermost thoughts spilled out for anyone to see. Women of any age, young, old, whatever their race or upbringing will find something that they can relate to. The gamut of emotions I went through with the character was astounding! Thank you for sharing you hardships, heartaches, and your triumphs with the literary world."

—Sherri Evola, Real Estate Consultant/Productivity Coach/ Marketing Specialist

"I couldn't put *Carnival Mirror* down. I was so captivated by her story! I anxiously read each 'self esteem' tip at the end of every chapter. *Carnival Mirror* helped me take a look at my own negative 'self-talk' and helped me rebuild my self esteem."

—Breanna Davis, Nutrition Club Owner

Carnival Mirror

Chelynne Nicole

PublishAmerica
Baltimore

ISBN: 1-60836-482-8 (softcover)
ISBN: 978-1-4489-1826-3 (hardcover)
PUBLISHED BY PUBLISHAMERICA, LLLP
www.publishamerica.com
Baltimore

Printed in the United States of America

I dedicate this book to every woman who has been abused by her husband or partner.

Acknowledgments

First and foremost, I'd like to thank and acknowledge my parents, John, and B. Alice, the two most caring and special parents I could ever have. Without them caring so much, I would not be here.

I would like to thank my children, Samantha and Matthew. You are my rocks. Thanks for recognizing that I was going down the wrong path and having the courage to tell me. Bre Bre, you are the best daughter-in-law anyone could have. Thanks to Ali for making my son so happy! Welcome to the family!

Special thanks goes to Carol, who told me I could write the book. She said, "Just sit down and start writing." I would also like to thank Sherri; she is one of the strongest women I have ever met. I have learned a lot from her.

I would also like to thank my cousin Carole. She has been supportive of me all my life, and she is very protective of me. Carole saw me through all 3 of my marriages. She has seen how far I have come.

To my sister Nancy, thank you for always being there when I need you and understanding why I had to tell my story.

My heart goes out to Laurie. Laurie has always believed in me. She has known me since my third marriage. When that marriage failed she was right there. She has laughed and cried with me. She has always told me I can do anything I set my mind to. Laurie is like my journal. I can tell her anything, kind of like "Dear Diary…."

I'd like to thank Leah, my life coach, friend, mentor, and confidante. You rock, Leah! Thanks for listening. Thanks for all the advice and direction. Thanks for being the catalyst towards my recovery. Thanks for telling me to date myself for a while. It worked. I am no longer afraid to be alone. I learned a lot about what I want in a partner, too!

A little thank you to my cat Missy for walking on my papers, chasing the papers coming out of the printer, walking on the keyboard, and putting her furry paw in my coffee. That was her way of telling me I needed to take a break.

I would also like to thank all the men that have come into my life in the last 7 years and shown me there are great men out there! Thanks to Tim, Tom, Tony, Cary, Randy, Stephen, John, Gregg, Gary, Doug, and last but not least, Paul.

Contents

Introduction

For the last 7 years I have been on a journey of repairing my soul that was abused—physically, mentally, and emotionally. I had three back-to-back abusive marriages in 26 years.

As you read my story you will see how low my self esteem was. You will also see the red flags I was too naive to see when choosing a partner. My journey is full of love, rejection, loss, fear, and so much pain that I am not sure where I found my strength. It was strength personified.

The decisions I made as a young teen to get married was the catalyst that started me on a landslide of self-destructive behavior due to abuse, which catapulted me into choosing two more wrong partners.

I have learned through the years that people with LSE (low self-esteem) tend to withdraw or isolate. They are usually unhealthy communicators. Relationships are greatly affected by this thinking disorder. Feelings of inadequacy will be with them constantly. Once LSE is formed, the fear and anxiety that accompanies it affects everything a person says and thinks.

Like me, many will become underachievers, feeling that they don't deserve any better in their lives. They will feel stuck. They tend to avoid initiating relationships, seeking a new job, or learning something new out of rejection or fear.

LSE starts when you are a child and begins from parents, child-care workers, teachers, grandparents, peers, siblings, and other relatives. Parents have the biggest influence on their children. They tend to grow up tolerating bad behavior, and they don't know whom they can trust or aren't able to identify when to trust.

As a child I believed I could do anything. When I reached middle school, once confident, I became suddenly aware that I didn't fit in or couldn't measure up, due to other kids forming cliques or putting me down. This compounds the LSE, and I found myself as a teen sitting alone feeling rejected. These feelings of rejection led to my bad life decisions.

Positive self-esteem gives you the courage to be your own person and make the right decisions. I wanted everyone to like me, but not if I had to give into any kind of peer pressure, and I never drank or did drugs. Positive self-esteem would have given me the strength and awareness to make the right decisions in choosing a partner. I did not value or respect myself, and I made bad decisions that have affected and will affect the rest of my life.

Chapter 1

Mirror, Mirror on the Wall

I can't escape my broken past. It is like looking in a carnival mirror. Every day the reflection stays with me with every step. Images, some clear, some not. But if you put them all together like a movie reel you would see three dysfunctional marriages full of abuse, lies, and the maneuverability to make you think you are the one going crazy.

Even as a child, I can remember thinking I couldn't do anything. I was afraid to jump off the diving board, I never did learn how to dive into a pool, I can't swim very well, and I never took up an instrument. All of this was because I felt I could not do it, which came from fear that I would fail if I tried.

When I was a little 12-year-old girl I can remember going to my mom in tears. Even at such a young age I hated who I was. I wanted to be someone else. No amount of play or fantasizing was ever enough. She said, "Who would you want to be? If you were anyone else you would not have me as your mom, your dad wouldn't be your dad, and your cat, Tramp wouldn't be here either," but the most important thing she said to me that stayed with me was, "You would not be you, and you need to be the best Chelynne that you can be." That has stayed with me for 37 years. Whenever I feel down and hate my life, I remember those words.

Why, you may ask, did I hate who I was? Even back in 1971 little girls looked at magazines of movie stars, and I can remember comparing myself to Leigh Taylor Young, a beautiful woman married to Ryan O'Neal. She had the most amazing eyes and complexion. I also remember idolizing Nancy Sinatra and Ann-Margaret. I would look in the mirror and see my eyes and face and wish I was beautiful.

I remember when I was a little girl watching Nancy Sinatra perform "These Boots Are Made for Walkin'" in her white go-go boots, and I thought, *Oh, if I just had a pair of those I would be beautiful just like Nancy Sinatra!* The next day I asked my mom and dad, and we went on the hunt to find the boots for me! I was so excited. We went from store to store looking for the boots. We finally found them, purchased them, and they were mine! I came home and opened my box and put on my boots and modeled them. I felt so beautiful and special. It was so exciting—though short-lived. While the go-go boots were on I valued myself and felt pride. Without the boots on I fell back to no longer feeling special.

I always felt better when I went outside to my fenced-in backyard. It was my safe haven. The smell of the honeysuckle covered the whole yard. I felt like I could do or be anyone I wanted to be in my back yard playground. I could be a beautiful princess and have my servants bring me tea, or I could be a beautiful, graceful ballerina and dance for everyone. Everyone would clap. Whoever I was, everyone loved me, and I was beautiful.

To this day, whenever I smell honeysuckle I am taken back to a playground in my backyard at a time when life was easy; there were no stress or big hurdles to overcome. I always felt overshadowed by the overwhelming feeling that whoever I was—I was not good enough. I wasn't the most beautiful princess or the most graceful ballerina.

I am not sure what it was I didn't like about my looks. I had long brown hair, brown eyes, and freckles on both cheeks. I had one dimple. I had very long legs and was good at broad jump and high jump. I was also good at the hula hoop and won an award for doing extraordinary things with it, like taking it from my ankle all the way up to my neck and back down to my ankle, pulling my foot out and hula hooping on one foot. However, I was not good in school. I did not have a good attention span, and this held me back. I was bored, too. I hated history. I always seemed to be in trouble at school for talking too much or disrupting the class.

My parents were in their mid 30s when I was born. My father was a pilot for a local airline and usually worked the graveyard shift, and my mother was a real-estate agent working the usual 9 to 5. However, I seem to remember a lot of overtime for my mother, and my father working a lot of holidays. My first memory was on Christmas when Santa brought me my Chatty Cathy Doll on roller skates when I was 3 years old. I remember dragging my doll from my tricycle, and I remember riding my bike without training wheels.

In second grade, I had to have surgery on my ears and have them pinned down, due to their sticking out. I endured names like "Dumbo," "Big Ears" and "Floppy" during my childhood. This caused to me isolate myself in my room a lot. I can remember playing with Barbies and playing my record player over and over.

I don't remember as a child ever taking a pretty picture. I felt ugly. My mom enrolled me in a modeling class when I was 12, and I learned how to be graceful and elegant. I had a lot of fun in the modeling class. There were modeling shows I modeled in for several months at the department store before I got bored and dropped out.

I was basically an only child. My mom's first husband died when my sister was 11. A few years later, my mom met my dad and had me. My sister and I were 16 years apart, and I didn't get along with her. She was too authoritative. She called my dad by his first name, and I never understood that. They fought all the time, each one trying to get his or her point across and neither one listening. It wasn't until I was about 10 that I was told that she did not have the same dad.

We lived in a small house in a good neighborhood filled with lots of kids to play with; however, I remember being alone a lot. All the little girls in the neighborhood had big brothers. I was so jealous. I wanted a big brother to lean on and have him stick up for me. We all played typical kid games. We would play kick-the-can until late in the evening until we heard our parents call our names. We played hot box, and I was always in the middle, due to my being very tall. Hot box was a game with two players with gloves who threw a baseball to each other, and the person in the middle tried to get it. I was best friends with Di, who lived around the corner and up the hill. We would meet at the corner and spend evenings together. Sometimes we would tell our moms that we were spending the night at each other's houses, and not go to either one and go to a boy's house in the neighborhood. We spent a lot of time playing in the cemetery, scaring each other. We had a lot of fun, laughing and pretending to be older than we were. I was also very close with my next door neighbors. Kara was a year older than me, and Cinda was a year younger than me. They went to a Catholic school, and I really only saw them in the evenings or on weekends. Our parents would take us to the movies, or we would spend an evening at the pool. They moved to a neighborhood about 10 miles away when I was 12.

Soon after we had new neighbors. Di and I watched as they moved in. All four kids were boys, and one looked to be about our age, and he was so cute! He soon became my first love. I was 13, and he was 11. His name was Brian. Eventually I became the family babysitter. I developed a crush on him because he was so cute and acted older than he was. I remember when we kissed for the first time. It was just a peck, but it meant a lot. A young summer romance, full of flirting and acting silly, like running around and catching fireflies, and him putting one down my shirt. We had a lot of fun that summer. We would sneak little kisses when we knew our parents weren't watching out the windows, or we would spend time at the pool dunking each other. We teased each other all the time. I could call him today, and we would talk for hours.

When I was 14, I had my first real date with Donnie. We went to the new, local amusement park. It was the first year of the park, and we got to sample all the food. His grandmother gave him $50, and he bought me a ring at the park. We ate pizza, rode the rides, and when he brought me home, he kissed me. We talked on the phone a few times after that, and then this little romance fizzled. He moved away a few months later.

In 1975, when I was 16, I met Jared at a basketball game. Jared was 19. He had a dark complexion and dark eyes, thick eyebrows, and a stance that at 6 feet tall said he was sure of himself and confident. Maybe a little too confident, almost coming across as cocky. He had long sideburns, too. His dark features, and good looks captivated me. He had very broad shoulders and looked like a football player.

I started going to all the basketball games and trying to sit by him. One night he offered me a ride home with him and his best friend

Brady. I knew him from school, so I was comfortable going with them. I had a friend with me, too, so she and I got in the car and we drove around with them listening to Ozark Mountain Daredevils. We loved their music.

We started dating and fell in love very quickly. We spent every day together. He would pick me up at school, and we would drive around, and he would come by my house and help me with homework. He was already out of school and spending the summer here with his family. They had just moved from South Dakota. We dated for about 6 months, and we grew to love each other very much. It wasn't long before it got serious. The day I skipped school and he took me sledding we stopped, and he bought me a mood ring. We had a lot of fun that day laughing, kissing, and talking about how we felt about each other. We would sit in the car and watch the mood ring change colors. We truly believed it had something to do with how we felt about each other when it would change colors.

On a dark, cold, snowy night sitting in the car, he kissed me and asked me to marry him. He presented me a beautiful heart-shaped diamond with two blue sapphires on each side. It was a beautiful engagement ring. My parents liked him, and they knew I was falling in love with him. He really seemed to care about me and love me. We got along very well. We told my parents that we were engaged, and they gave me their consent, which was better than my running off. We decided he would join the Marine Corps, and we looked forward to our future.

Esteem Yourself!

Set goals. Even small ones. This will build your confidence and self-esteem.

Chapter 2

Ring Toss

In a week's time we planned a small wedding in front of his grandpa's fireplace at their lake house. My best friend Di was my bridesmaid. She wore a lavender print dress, and I wore a long white dress. The flowers were lavender and pink carnations. We had a small rehearsal dinner at a local restaurant that had a fireplace in the corner. The ambiance was perfect. It was a beautiful place and offered good food.

We got married in spring of 1976. The wedding was very small, just relatives and a few friends. I remember the vows and I thought we would be together the rest of our lives. After we were married we had a 10-day honeymoon. The first two nights we spent at a local hotel. After that we just enjoyed each other's company, opening presents and planning our future. With his plan to join the Marine Corps and have a career, we were excited, wondering where we would end up living.

After a week we started getting him packed to leave for Marine-Corps boot camp. The morning he was supposed to fly out he was taking a shower, I grabbed a big plastic cup full of ice water and threw it over the top of the shower. He screamed from the shock and opened up the shower door and looked at me, shivering and laughing.

He asked, "Why did you do that?"

I said, "I just want you to know how much I will miss you!"

He knew I liked to play practical jokes. He started chasing me naked through the house to get me back! We always played like that!

I saw him off at the airport; tears filled my eyes as the plane took off. The first few days were grueling waiting for letters. I would get up and go to school, think about him all day, and not concentrate on schoolwork at all. Then the days turned into weeks. I was so lonely I cried every day and night. I missed him so much it hurt! Getting out of bed was unbearable, knowing I had to go to school and try to concentrate. My first letter finally came.

Dear Chelynne, I miss you so much, your touch, and your kiss. I can't wait to get home...

We wrote each other every day but it took days to get the mail. I loved getting his letters and feeling connected to him. I loved knowing about his days away from me.

After about 10 weeks I got a letter saying he had hurt his back. Two weeks later he received an honorable discharge. All his dreams were crushed. He was very upset. He came home about a week later. I was so happy to see him! We hugged and kissed! He was glad to be back home. Several days later we settled into our new little apartment.

We immediately started having struggles with bills, paying for groceries, car troubles, and just stupid arguments where no one would win. I saw Jared's temper for the first time. It was scary. We got in an argument about the blow dryer. I guess he got it aimed at him while he was combing his hair, and I thought he was going to hit me with it. He grabbed it in a huff and jerked it to where it unplugged!

I was frightened and shocked, but he was always so sorry for being angry and promised never to scare me like that again. After awhile he became very jealous and possessive. He kept accusing me of having an affair, but I just thought he was feeling insecure. I felt sorry for him. I believed I could change him. Then he turned against my family and friends and tried not to let me see them.

I thought his attacks on me must somehow be my fault. I found myself asking, *What have I done to deserve this? Why am I making him so mad that he has to treat me this way?* I couldn't bring myself to tell anyone what was happening. I was embarrassed and couldn't help thinking it was my fault.

It became evident that I needed to start working. I made a decision, and I quit school the first month of my senior year and went to work for a dress shop. He worked at a men's clothing store and found work part-time as a mechanic.

Struggling to be a housewife, I was trying to learn how to cook, keep a clean house, do laundry, and spend time alone, due to Jared working so many hours. I asked him if we could get a puppy to keep me company. We went looking that following weekend, and I saw a little, pure-black dog with a long tail. He seemed to like me right from the start. I named him Cupid and took him home. It wasn't long before Cupid was part of the family. He was lovable, and he followed me around all day.

One day we left him outside on a leash because it was so nice outside. The apartment neighbors didn't seem to mind. He was lovable, and the kids would pet him all the time.

We came home that day, and I opened the back sliding glass door. Cupid was lying dead in a box on the back porch with a note that read, "I am so sorry; a rock hit him from the lawnmower." I was upset, crying, and felt like I lost my best friend. Jared, did not know how to make it better. He was so angry that someone would put Cupid in a box rather than covering him up and coming and telling us.

I started dreading spending time alone again while Jared was working, and I was sad that Cupid was not there to be my buddy. It took a long time to get over my little buddy.

After we had been married about 8 months Jared, received a letter from a lady in North Dakota he used to have a relationship with. She sent a picture of a baby boy and said it was his. He flew to see her and find out more about the child. I never felt like he told me the truth. He never said whether the child was his or not. We fought for months about that.

A few months later we moved into a small house that we rented while we saved money. Jared fixed cars and painted houses for extra money on the weekends and his days off. One day when I got in the car to go to the store, I found a lipstick on the floor of the car in the back seat. The lipstick was not mine. My first thought was that he was having an affair with a lady whose car he worked on. He talked me out of it by telling me that since he had her car and was working on it, she needed him to take her somewhere. I think this is the first time he cheated on me. I never found out for sure.

The rest of the years with him were turbulent, to say the least. He always made passes at my girl-friends, and he was a totally different person at home with just me. I have blocked a lot of it out due to how painful it all was, and I was just a young woman going through this. He went from a caring, loving man to a hateful, controlling, womanizing abuser. Jared was cunning. When he hit me, he was always careful never to mark my face. He always aimed for my chest or thighs.

One day we went to a local discount store. We fought before we went; we fought on the way, too. When we got there, I decided I did not want to go in and be anywhere near him. He jerked me out of the car, and I hit the concrete, and we were rolling around in the parking lot, each one trying to gain control; I was trying to get free, and he was trying to keep me penned. I can't even imagine what we looked like, rolling around on the concrete at a public place. No one called the police or anything. I am not sure what made us quit fighting, but I was glad to be up off the concrete. We got in an argument on the way home—he took my house keys and was holding them, taunting me. I went to grab for them, slipped, and gave him a bloody nose. He was livid. He pulled the car over and ordered me to get out! It was a busy highway, so I talked him out of it, apologizing over and over.

One year we decided to take a vacation and go to the lake. We got in an argument because I wanted to stop and take a break, and he was always in a hurry. He got mad and he pulled over and pulled me out of the car and left me there! I had no idea where I was. I was on a gravel part of the side of the highway. I had to walk, make a phone call, and get a taxi and take a train home. I was too embarrassed to tell anyone that my husband left me on the side of the road. The next time I rode in a car with him he put his hand on my shoulder and roughly pushed my face up against the glass window and said, "I decide where we go, and if you get out and join me or not."

I wanted out, but I didn't know how to get out. I was scared.

Five years into the marriage, we had a baby girl. We named her

Samantha. She was so cute with dark hair that stood straight up. Jared had a house built for us on a small plot of land. We moved in right after Samantha was born. Samantha started sleeping through the night almost immediately. When she was 3 months old I was baking cookies in the kitchen and doubled over in pain. I ended up in the emergency room, and was told I had to have surgery for a ruptured cyst on my ovary. Jared took good care of Samantha while I was in the hospital. When I got out of the hospital a few days later, I couldn't get around very well, and had to take time off to recuperate. One day, Jared got bored and he left and took the battery out of my car so I couldn't leave. He left me with no milk and no diapers. I was furious with him! I remember when he came home and said he met a woman named "Tara," and she wanted to take him to a "ball" game. He chuckled, knowing what kind of game she really wanted. He started spending more and more nights out late. I was so lonely. His best friend, Pat, came by one night to check on me. He hated the way Jared treated me. Pat held me in his arms and he kissed me very passionately. I wanted him. I wanted comfort. Jared had hurt me deeply. But he was his best friend. He said he would call and check on me later.

A few months later we separated and Jared moved out for awhile. Pat came over for dinner and tried to make love to me, but I still wouldn't let him. I was angry at the way Jared had treated me, and now I didn't trust any man. I spent that summer taking my daughter to the lake, and Pat would meet us there. He told me he was in love with me. I was so numb I couldn't feel anything. We never did have a physical relationship, but he was on my mind a lot. He was so good to me, but he was Jared's best friend.

That Fall Jared moved back in. I foolishly thought things would get better now that we were back together. The day I got proof of the affair was just an ordinary day. I got up and drank some coffee, got my daughter up out of bed, and a friend of mine came over.

Jared said, "How about I give you gals money to go to the amusement park?"

What? He never offered money for anything. I knew he had something in mind and was getting me out of the way. He left, and we decided to forgo the amusement park and drive around. We were driving down a two-lane road, and I saw his car coming our direction. I saw the cowboy hat, his blue shirt, and a little blonde in the passenger's seat of his specially painted 1980 Firebird. We turned around and tried to catch up. We lost him. When we got back home, there he was, sitting, watching football and drinking a beer, in different clothes like he had been back for a long time. Nope, not quite Jared. I went and looked in the clothes hamper and found the blue shirt. The cowboy hat was on the bed. I accused him, and he said I was crazy, that wasn't him. He said he had been home for about two hours.

The next day I was on a mission to find this woman. I remembered her name from when he told me about her. I found out she lived not too far from me, just a couple towns over. I went to a gas station and asked if anyone knew a girl named "Tara" that was a nurse and went after married men. They knew right off who I was looking for and pointed me to her house. As I drove up, there was Jared's car. I banged on the front door as hard as I could, and I was yelling his name. He finally came to the door. I could see her standing behind him, scantily dressed. It made me ill. He said he was getting a bid to paint her house. He always had an excuse.

He had been having an affair for several months. He knew I was hurt and ended the affair, or so I thought. A few weeks later, Jared had an appendicitis attack. Tara was a nurse at a local hospital.

I said, "You better not end up on her floor."

Well, he did. I walked in his room, and there she was, on duty, by his bedside. I was livid. I asked her to leave and to get another nurse. She said this was her floor and her patient. I immediately went down to the administrator's office. I said, "If you don't keep that woman out of my husband's room, you will read in tomorrow morning's paper that your nurses are giving their patients blow jobs!"

She knew I was dead serious. She said, "Well, I can keep her out of there during normal business hours, but I can't keep her out of the hospital after hours."

I said okay. I was still upset. I walked in his room that evening after hours, and there she was. I said, "Step out into the hall." It was time for us to have it out. I asked, "Why do you insist on seeing my husband?" He has me, and he has a daughter."

She said she loved him and she couldn't stay away.

I said, "Please leave him alone," and walked off.

A year later I decided I could not take any more of his abuse—physical or emotional, and his cheating. So I decided to pack my bags. He begged me to stay. He said, "Let's move to Wyoming and start over," and he said he ended the affair.

I stayed due to we had a daughter, and I did still love him. I realize now I didn't love me enough. We arranged to have his father live in our house, and we packed up and moved to Wyoming. His mother and sister lived there, so we stayed with them until we found our own place. After about a month of living in Wyoming we bought our own small ranch. Jared would take off on weekends saying he was looking for work in other cities, but I knew something was going on. I was starting to put the pieces together one day that he was cheating, but I would never in my life have imagined what I would find and who it would point to.

One day he was out with the cattle at the ranch, and I went out to the truck to search for some things I was missing in the move. I looked under the floor board and found a box. In the box were letters. I grabbed one of the letters and tore it open and started to read.

Dear Jared,

and I turned the page over to see who it was from. Oh my God! These were love letters Tara and Jared had written to each other. He had not ended the affair! Tara had moved to Montana, and to be closer to her and keep me he moved us to Wyoming and traveled there. I immediately packed up our daughter and flew home. When he got home he found me at my mom's, and I was alone in the house. Samantha was with my parents at dinner. I heard the car door shut, and he started pounding on the front door. I was immediately scared for my life. I ran to the back bedroom. He swung open the door and knew instantly my parents weren't home, and he proceeded come back to the bedroom where I was and started screaming and cussing. He swung and hit me in the face. This was the first time he ever hit me in the face. He hit me so hard that my glasses went flying, and I hit the floor hard. I stayed down, and he left.

Esteem Yourself!
Think positive.

Chapter 3

The Juggling Act

After I gained composure, I stood back up and looked in the mirror. I had a black eye, and my cheek was all red and puffy. I put on my sunglasses and some makeup to cover the redness. As I sat there looking in the mirror, I started putting a plan together to start looking for an apartment. My daughter was now two years old. I found out about another affair while I was looking for an apartment. I ran into a high school friend who knew Jared also. I told her I was looking for an apartment for my daughter and me. She said, "I don't blame you. If my husband was having an affair with his best friend's sister I would move out, too." I looked at her, and I should have looked more shocked, but I wasn't. I immediately figured out it was Ciera, a pretty, petite blonde, 6 years younger than he was.

One day I was in the kitchen of our house, and I was making dinner. I couldn't find Jared anywhere. I finally went downstairs, and Ciera was in my garage standing next to him. She said, "Tell her, Jared, tell her that you love me."

He wouldn't say anything. He kissed her and made her leave. Before she left, she looked me in the eye and said, "I want Jared, his kids, a BMW, and a $300,000 house."

I started running into them when I would go into the city. She hated me, because I was still married to him, and I hated her for sleeping with him. We had words many times. The most memorable occasion was at my daughter's birthday skating party. She was there, and I was furious with Jared for bringing her. As soon as I confronted Jared she was in my face. She was verbally attacking me so hard that I took a swing at her, only to be grabbed by Jared, who ended up getting decked in the face by my hand! Yeah, he deserved it!

I could not find an apartment that I could afford on my own, so I continued to live in the house with Jared. I remember one time he had come home from seeing Ciera, and I was getting ready to take a shower and he forced me with an M-16 infantry assault rifle pointed at my head to have sex with him every way he wanted. He knew I was leaving him, but he still wanted us both. The very next day, my parents loaned me money for an apartment that was based on my income as secretary, and I moved out.

One evening in our new apartment I was at home wallpapering the living room, and my daughter was with her father. I received a box. In the box, were all my things from the house with a note from Ciera. She had packed my things! Who knows what she kept for herself. What a bitch!

That evening there was a knock on the door. It was Jared. He had come to "discuss" child support. We got in an argument, and he knocked me down. He flipped my back over his back, and when I landed, I landed with such a jolt it took my breath away. He immediately put his weight on me and put his hands around my neck and started choking me. I was about to black out, but I wasn't going to let him kill me. His weight was right on me, and I was no match for him so I kicked the ladder. It startled him just enough that when he turned around I made a run for it and ran out of the apartment and up the stairs and called the police. As he always did, he talked his way out of getting arrested. He could talk his way out of anything. I got a restraining order against him that next day. My back was injured. It hurt badly. I could barely walk without having to sit down. Every day since, I have had to baby my back and can no longer do certain things, like ride a sled or a jet ski without pain. Ciera moved into my house and took over everything. She was now living in the house that Jared and I had built for our lives.

A few months later, when my daughter was 2 ½, we were driving down a two-lane road, and when I got over the hill, there was a car stopped, completely in my lane. I slammed on the brakes, skidded to the left, and the car died. Before I could get it started I could hear squealing tires over the hill. I knew we were going to be rear-ended. I laid down on Samantha to protect her in her car seat. At the moment of impact, my back flipped around and hit the dash. I felt pain immediately! Now my back-injury from the abuse was worse from the car wreck.

I was taken by ambulance to the hospital, immediately put in traction, and was in awful pain. I was actually hanging by cords in the air to keep my back straight. I had two ruptured discs. I spent ten days in the hospital. I wore a back brace for 9 months under my clothes. I was put on light duty at work. Eventually I was let go from the job because I couldn't stand up very long and unpack the inventory without pain. I was really injured and had to baby my back for a long time. I did everything to avoid back surgery. My daughter and I moved in with my parents, and I found a job as a secretary. I was able to sit and type or file, and this was a lot easier on my back.

Two years later, Samantha, was 4 by this time, we finally got our own apartment and settled in nicely. It was right before Christmas, and Jared came over to put a bicycle together for Alisa. We were getting along better, and his restraining order had expired. He had on some new cowboy boots. I made a comment about them, and he said Ciera got them for him; "we are engaged!" Before we were divorced he was engaged! He even tried to get me in bed that night. He kept trying to see her and me at the same time. He called Ciera from my apartment and lied to her about his whereabouts.

Finally, in 1985, our divorce became final. He started calling me and telling me to meet him at a hotel, and he would give me some money if I slept with him. He was not paying child support, and I was desperate for the money, but not enough to sleep with him. Three weeks later he married Ciera He called me the night before they got married from his rehearsal dinner and said he couldn't go through with it, said he still loved me. I said, "You are going to marry this woman, after all the hell you put me through!"

I felt relieved, finally. Relieved and alone.

Soon after the "finality" of the divorce I started going out with friends to bars and meeting men. I was angry, hurt, and my pride was crushed. One night I was so depressed after a couple of drinks I left the bar alone and drove home. As I was driving, I had this overwhelming sadness hit me. I was upset to go home to an empty house. All of a sudden I sped up on this two-lane road. I took the short-cut home that I had taken many times. The speed limit was 35, and I was speeding up to 45, 55, 65, and 70. At that point I wished I had a brick wall to crash in to. I did not want to live! I felt abused—used, crushed under a shoe. I could barely look people in the eye! I was picturing all the hitting, pushing, and yelling I had endured, and the final blow was when he left me for Ciera and was engaged before we were even divorced! I was so angry that he had hit me where no one could see it. He always hit me in the chest and shoulders. No one could ever see the bruises but me. I lived with those bruises. I looked at them. I felt shattered in pieces like broken glass. After that night, I pulled myself together and decided to stay out of the bars and put the pieces of my life back together.

Shortly after that I got sick, really sick. I had a terrible strep throat. I hadn't eaten, hadn't had any water or anything. I stopped by my mom and dad's and literally passed out on the stairs, just fell over from being so weak. My dad took me to the only hospital that would take me in on such a low income. I remember being in the waiting room on a Gurney. I was between a gunshot victim and a knife victim. I did not want to live. I was so weak. My dad brought my daughter in the room after I was examined. I remember she looked at me with those big eyes and smiled and told me she loved me. At that moment, I decided I would live for her. I started crying, and I knew she needed me.

Esteem Yourself!
Laugh daily.

Chapter 4

Smoke 'n' Mirrors

After the year mark of being divorced, I joined a local singles group. I started going to the meetings and parties. One night in 1986, I was in a small town not far from home at a singles party. I saw the most amazingly handsome man. My heart felt alive. He had a smile and a laugh that was so contagious, I found myself just staring at him. He asked me to slow dance, and we danced to Madonna's, "Crazy for You." His name was Daniel. He had blonde hair, blue eyes, and he had a stocky build. He had such a nice touch holding one hand and having the other on my lower back while we were dancing. He kept telling me things that made me laugh. I loved that he could make me laugh! We started seeing each other at meetings and parties. We would take off after the meetings and get a bite to eat and just sit and talk. One day I was at work, and he called and asked me to take the afternoon off and meet him at a local hotel. I jumped at the chance to take off the afternoon and relax at a hotel with Daniel. We had an amazing afternoon. After we made love we lay there and talked about everything. He joked a lot, and I enjoyed laughing. We saw each other after that for several months. He lived about 45 minutes away, and we had a hard time fitting each other in. But there were lots of meetings and parties to go to see each other if we hadn't been able to schedule it. He told me had been separated for months and headed for divorce. We saw each other for several months. We went out of town together and spent weekends on the lake. We had a lot of fun at a resort about 4 hours from home. We played tennis, ice skated, danced. It was great.

A few months after that, I went out of town to a convention. I went with a couple other ladies that I didn't know very well. They told me they had booked rooms for all of us. Well, when we got there, 7 hours later I found out I did not have a room. There was a mix up and they were booked solid. One of the men there, Robert, said, it was okay, I could sleep in the hospitality suite after everyone was done partying. He was actually staying at the hotel next door and asked me to go over with him to have a drink. When we got over there, he handed me a drink and asked me up to his room.

I said, no. We headed back to the hotel where the convention was going on. The hospitality suite had a lot of people running around, drinking beer from the kegs, and mixing their own drinks. I got a little too drunk that night. I did end up sleeping in the hospitality suite. That next morning, I woke up, and there was the weight of someone on top of me! It was Robert.

"Oh, my God! What are you doing?" I rolled him off of me and I ran to the bathroom. There was a knock on the door, and he said, "Hold on a minute; there is a lady in here."

He just acted like it was normal that he was in bed with me, like, since I used his hospitality suite and he had the key, he would just make himself at home and take advantage of my being drunk. Later on that day, he grabbed my arm and walked me to be introduced me to his fiancée. I still get ill when I think of it. There was nothing I could do.

I had put myself in that situation and got drunk on top of it. That is the one and only time I was ever drunk. I learned my lesson.

When I got back in town, I was talking to Daniel. I told him what happened. He was hurt, angry, and wondered why I didn't do anything. I tried to explain that I had put myself in that situation and that I was very sorry. He said he loved me and did not want anyone to hurt me, and he felt bad that he had not been there. It took awhile to mend things with Daniel. He was hurt.

One night a few weeks later we met for dinner and went to a local park. We talked and he held my face and kissed me tenderly. He said, "I am falling in love with you."

I said, 'I feel the same."

We sat there and talked about our future, made plans to see each other again, and he kissed me goodbye. I went home so happy and full of hope for the future with this man. I was so in love.

The very next morning he called and said, "I am so sorry; I can't do this." When I got home last night my wife and daughter were worried sick, and I can't do this to them. I am so sorry."

"What? Wife and daughter? Not separated?"

He said he was still living there to gain information because she was cheating on him with his best friend.

"Oh my God, but I love you."

He ended the call with "I am so sorry, I love you, too."

It took months to get over Daniel. To this day, I still feel like he was the love of my life. When my daughter was 7, three years after Daniel and I ended it, I took her to a Haunted House in the same town Daniel lived in. I was prepared to run into him, but I was not prepared for his new life. When we were walking up to the long, flat warehouse building that had been made into a haunted house, I saw a creature dressed in green wearing a mask. It looked like "swamp thing." He took off his mask, and it was Daniel. We hugged, said hi, and he said, "Go meet my wife. She is taking tickets. Her name is Cathy."

Well, his first wife was named Cynthia, so it hit me right then and there he divorced and married someone else. As we stood in line, my eye caught sight of the woman taking the tickets. It was like looking in a mirror. She had my hair color, my body shape, my glasses, my dimples, and my eyes! They say everyone has a twin, and I just met mine face to face. Oh, my God, if I hadn't seen it, I would never have believed it! I can't begin to put it into words how it felt knowing the man I loved, divorced his wife and married a woman that looked so much like me—it was like the universe was on a tilt. *This can't be real.* I felt like I was in a dream. A few years later I heard he divorced Cathy and married a young girl in town, had two more kids, and is now a stay-at-home dad. He is now 56. When I knew him he was 33, and I was 26. We felt like teenagers. I saw him through the years at local fireworks shows and festivals. We always hugged and caught each other up on our lives. The last time I saw him was four years ago. My heart still skipped a beat. I saw him in a newspaper the other day, and he looked very happy with his young wife and two kids. I still wish it had been with me.

In 1988 I met Rocco. I was told about him from a friend. She asked If I minded writing letters to him, because he just moved here. He had gotten in some trouble and was staying with his brother. He was very lonely. We started writing letters to each other. After two months I went to meet him.

Down the stairs came a man unlike any I have ever known. He was tall, lanky, with dark hair, tattoos on his arms, and dark eyes. He had on a fitted dark-blue tee shirt with short sleeves, and faded jeans with slashes torn in the knees. He barely looked at me and lit up a cigarette. He had this quiet, cocky air about him. I was suddenly attracted to this mysterious bad boy.

We started spending weekends at his dad's out in the country. We tackled projects like fixing the fence, repairing the roof, painting, and I learned all about farm animals. Being out in the country gave me a chance to learn new things. I even started making fresh bread and home-made cinnamon rolls. Yes, I was settling into country life quite nicely. We would get in water-fights and paint fights and laugh and chase each other around the house. We were in love, and it showed to anyone around us.

After a few months he asked me to marry him. We decided on December 15, which was 5 months away and the exact day he would get off of probation.

We got married at my aunt's house. I wore a knee-length, lace-and-pink two-piece dress. It was very pretty with silver heels. I wore a pink-and-silver flower in my hair. He wore a black tux with a white shirt. The ceremony went pretty fast, and then it was time for the reception that we had right there at the house. We sipped on punch and took pictures of us tastefully feeding each other cake. It was a lot of fun. I was really happy! A friend sent a limo for us, and we took off for our honeymoon at a country resort about 20 miles away. It was a really rustic place out in the country. It had big, four-poster beds, soft, fluffy comforters, with tall ceilings in the cabins. We spent our honeymoon ordering food in, and then we would venture out to one of the walking paths and talk about our future. We checked out two days later and found a house to rent. It was a 3-bedroom split-level with a finished basement. I loved the red-brick front.

I settled in nicely as a new wife and started decorating, unpacking, and making plans. His transformation began slowly and was almost unnoticeable. It started out with a couple beers at night. Soon I started noticing a pipe and a bag of drugs. This progressed into a 6-pack of beer a night and a shortage of money due to his buying drugs weekly. He became more controlling and angry.

For Valentine's Day he got me a beautiful tennis bracelet. He threw the box at me and said, "Here, Bitch, Happy Valentine's Day!"

I got him a watch and he scolded me for two hours about how I spent too much money on it. I tried to explain I got it on sale, but that only escalated the fight.

One night I was in the kitchen getting something out of the freezer, and all of a sudden the freezer door slammed hard, so hard it shook everything in the refrigerator. He had karate kicked it because he said I kept it open too long just looking for something. That was the beginning of the end. He started getting bossier and watching my every move as time went on. After five months, our fights escalated, more money was gone, and he was up to a case of beer every 3 days.

On top of his controlling me, he hated all my friends. He always told me I was trying to live in a fantasy world. At that time, I would have rather lived anywhere than there. Around this time I started feeling strange from all the stress, being controlled and all the chaos, and went to see the doctor. On the way to the doctor's office I felt like all the traffic was closing in on me. I felt paranoid that the cars way behind me were coming up too close. I felt threatened at every turn. The doctor put me on a low dose anti-anxiety medicine, which helped a lot during the day and helped me sleep better, too.

It was Friday night and I wanted to go out and relax after a long week, but Rocco had plans to go hang out with his drug buddies. That is what I called them. I had nothing in common with them, and I am sure he talked bad about me when he was with them. He seemed to have grown to hate me. I ended up going out with a girlfriend. I stopped by Mom and Dad's on my way home and called Rocco around 11 p.m. He said he had been home awhile. I could tell he was drunk by the slur of his words. They still haunt me to this day. He had a bad attitude on the phone, too. He was gunning for me. We got in an argument, and I was afraid to go home.

He said, "Get home now."

I said, "I think I will just stay here for the night and see you in the morning."

He said, "If you don't come home now I will burn everything you own."

I said, "You would not do that; you love me."

He said, "Try me."

I was afraid to go home so I settled in at Mom and Dad's for the night. My daughter was with her dad for the weekend, so I didn't have to worry about her.

Esteem Yourself!

When someone compliments you, say, "Thank you." It is your compliment. Take it.

Chapter 5

Ring of Fire

The next morning the phone rang, and my dad answered it. It was the local police. They were telling my dad to prepare me for when I went home. My dad took me home, trying to explain what the officer said. I couldn't comprehend completely what I would drive up on. As we drove up, we saw a 6 ' x 6 ' burn mark in the side yard. My husband had set everything I owned out on the front lawn, lit a match, and it went up in smoke, my entire life's possessions! As I went running through the house my closet was empty, my drawers dumped out, pictures gone, mementos gone, and all the clothes my mom and sister had made me through the years, my daughter's baby dresses I had saved in boxes—gone! My mom had knitted beautiful sweaters on her electronic knitting machine, and my sister always made me beautiful skirts to wear with boots in the winter. She even once made me lace bras and underwear. I wanted to keep everything they had made for me. It was very precious to me. As I searched it was more evident that everything I cherished was gone. I was in shock, out of breath, deflated, violated, hurt. I was an incomplete shell of a woman left standing in the only thing I now owned, a tee shirt, pair of shorts, and flip-flops.

To this day I am not sure what all I lost in that fire. It was too much, too overwhelming to think about. I never talked about it, and this is the first time I have ever put it in print.

I left and filed for divorce. The judge granted the divorce, and Rocco had to pay a payment per month until the value of my possessions was paid off. He resented me horribly for that.

Shortly after I left a friend of mine that I met at work, Gina, a few years older than me, started going places with me. We went to antique malls, shopping, and I leaned on her a lot. She was my rock there for a while. We would talk about everything. She was really sweet, and she had a daughter who was pregnant and due in a few months. She even got the salesmen at work to put money in to help me buy clothes. I ended up with $500 and was able to buy new clothes to wear to work, and back in 1989 that went pretty far.

A few weeks later I was at her house. Suddenly I felt pain and doubled over. I ended up in the hospital and the doctor confirmed that I was 6 weeks pregnant and lost it. It was a very sad time. To cheer me up she got tickets for the Bon-Jove concert at the outdoor amphitheater. We went with two men she knew. On the way there they pulled over and got out the grain alcohol and green Kool-Aid mixture they had made. I wasn't much of a drinker, but I took a little bit to be social. We had a good time at the concert; little did I know how the good times would end.

I ran into Rocco with a young brunette at the concert. I told him about the miscarriage, and he seemed sad, but I didn't care. After the concert, Gina, the two guys, and I had a long walk to the car. Gina seemed winded, and sat down on the way a couple times. I hit her over the head with my poster and teasingly called her "Granny," and told her to speed it up. She was drunk, really drunk. On the way home she passed out in the back seat as we waited for traffic to clear.

When we got to our destination she was still passed out and got carried to a different car for the rest of the way home. The next morning, I was at work and I got a phone call. Gina was dead. I couldn't believe it; she was drunk but fine, when we dropped her off. I took the day off and cried all day. I prepared for the funeral, and her parents were calling me a lot because I was the last person to see her that they trusted. It was very sad. She was their only daughter. They ended up giving me all her clothes. That was so nice of them. That really helped me.

After the funeral I was a wreck. I took a Valium and slept for two days. When I woke up, I was still the same woman, who had a miscarriage, lost everything in a deliberate fire set by my husband, and lost my best friend from drinking at a concert. After 3 weeks, we got the results of the autopsy and some information I didn't even know. Her blood alcohol level was very high; they found marijuana and cocaine in her system. Her doctor said she had a heart murmur, and he had wanted her on a heart monitor that weekend. She told the doctor she would wear it after the concert and not before or during. She told no one, and now she was dead. They played the song, "You Are the Wind Beneath My Wings" at the funeral. I think of her often, and when I hear that song, I am taken back to all the fun we had, and how she entered my life when I needed someone most. I realize she is one of those people who enter your life for a short time to help you through something, and they are gone. She was an angel to me. Her parents sent me cards and letters, and I tried to keep in contact with them, but eventually we lost touch.

After the divorce became final, my daughter, now 9 years old, and I settled into our own apartment. Getting unpacked was a blur. I don't remember much because I was in such a deep depression. I remember living on the couch after work and on weekends. I don't know how I even worked at that time, looking back. I didn't even have the energy or desire to do anything.

I went to the doctor, and he put me on Xanax. It numbed me out for hours at a time. I took it at night and on weekends. I told the doctor I was so depressed that I didn't even want to fill the ice cube trays.

He said, "Go home, and tomorrow get up and fill one of them."

I got up the next morning and filled one of them. It felt pretty good to actually follow through on something so trivial. The next day, I got up, put on some sweats, threw my hair in a ponytail and actually walked outside of the apartment and stood by the pond. It was nice watching the geese. It was so cold, though, I didn't last long. Each day I would try something more. After about six months of living in a complete fog and being depressed, lonely, and quiet, I came out of it for my daughter. I realized I had missed her softball games and had been emotionally unavailable for weeks at a time. I started counseling, which helped with all the loss I had been through.

I made a friend in the complex, too. His name was Paul, and he would have me over for dinner, and if I needed any kind of maintenance done he would do it for me. He was really nice. He liked me, but I wasn't ready for any kind of dating. We became good friends. He kept me from being so lonely when my daughter would go to her dad's house. A few months later, Paul moved out into a house. I didn't know anyone else in the complex.

Esteem Yourself!

If you have the blues, that is one thing. If you are depressed, recognize it, and take control of it.

Chapter 6

Step Right Up!

As the fall came in, my loneliness got worse. My daughter was spending more time with her father and stepmom, and I didn't have any prospects for a new boyfriend or any friends at this time. Soon winter was closing in, and the holidays weren't far behind. I put up a small tree with what little money I had and got some things for my daughter. I loved filling her stocking with candy canes and little trinkets. It never really mattered what I got her for Christmas, her dad would always outdo me. He would show his love with material things.

Christmas came and went, and my depression and loneliness worsened. I was sitting on the edge of the bed on New Year's Eve and was so alone and sad. I put on my best tight jeans, heels, and a sweater, dabbed on my favorite perfume, and headed out the door. Next thing I knew I was in the car driving, not sure where I was going.

I pulled up to Rocco's apartment, not even thinking of all the hell he put me through. I just wanted to be held by someone familiar and not feel lonely. We rang in the New Year with fresh fruit, chips and chocolates, but no alcohol. Rocco had lost his license from too many DUIs. I spent the night, and we got up and made French toast together. I started spending more and more time with the man he was when I first fell in love with him. When he wasn't drinking he was a lot of fun. I still wasn't thinking about everything he had done to me. I was enjoying feeling needed and loved again.

Three weeks later I realized I was pregnant. I told Rocco, and we thought about it and decided to get married again. The months I was pregnant were fun months. We got an apartment together and went swimming a lot and even went camping. When I reached 7 months, the baby tried to come early, and the doctor put me on bed rest. One day I craved something sweet, and Rocco made French toast sticks out of hot dog buns. I thought that was so sweet. He did have a charming side. We got along great. I was on bed rest for the rest of the pregnancy. I got bored a lot and leaned on Rocco to tell me jokes, bring me magazines, and rent movies for me.

As soon as our baby boy was born we named him Matthew. Rocco was so happy, taking pictures, laughing, and passing out cigars. But his mood changed the day we brought him home.

He held me up against the wall, dropped his voice and said in a chilling voice, "You will never have him; he will never be yours."

Rocco left me that night, my first night home, and went to a concert. He did not get home until the next day. When I asked him where he was, he said he was with a friend and stayed out all night to keep him out of trouble. I resented him horribly for leaving me alone the first night we brought our baby boy home.

When Matthew was 4 months old, I picked him up from day care, and he had a slight fever. His fever spiked through the night, and I was really worried. That next day, Rocco went to work, and I called my dad. Dad took us to the doctor. The doctor looked at Matthew and said, "Get to the hospital right now." His fever had spiked again and he appeared lifeless.

My dad got us a police escort, and we rushed to the hospital, and we did not waste any time! On the way to the hospital I looked back at my baby in the car seat, and he was white as a ghost. We got to the hospital, and I carried him in and walked in front of everyone in line. I handed my almost lifeless baby boy to the doctor. I said, "My baby better be okay."

The doctor said, "I will do what I can."

I said, "No, you will do more than that!" I was totally beside myself. I called Rocco to tell him the bad news. Matthew had Meningitis. The first 48 hours were crucial. Rocco got to the hospital, and we kept an eye on Matthew every second. Waiting was excruciating! He was not getting better after the first 12 hours. We paced the floors, cried, and prayed for hours. The doctor called us into a room and told us to go home and prepare for his funeral.

This could not be happening! My baby was not going to die! I got home and got down on my knees. I prayed and cried. I screamed and cried. I was beyond consolation. We went back to the hospital and got good news! He was getting better after being on the medicine for 18 hours. Within days, he started getting his color back, then he smiled and got his appetite back. Finally! After 10 days of being in the hospital he finally got to come home.

Esteem Yourself!
Be present. Live in the moment.

Chapter 7

The Incredible Shrinking Woman

A few months later Rocco started building us a house. He would not let me have any say in any of the planning or anything. He wouldn't even build a window seat for me. At that point I lost interest in the house and this made Rocco very angry. After living being so controlled, so de-valued, and knowing I had put myself in this situation again, I was suicidal. I would imagine ending my life and not being around anymore. I had had so much abuse in my life from men I loved I didn't have anything else to give anyone. We had moved in with his dad out in the country, and I had no support system of any kind. I had no friends or anything. I was so isolated. I spent my days baking, doing laundry, and staring out the window. It was so quiet. I was 60 miles from home out in the country. I think he enjoyed keeping me so isolated. Once a week, I would go to the grocery store with Matthew. We would go to a restaurant to eat, and I would try to take my time. I hated going home. When we got home, Rocco grabbed the receipt from the groceries and demanded the change. I had spent it at the restaurant. He was furious! That next day I made a phone call to a suicide hot line. They got information from me, and called my doctor. I was told to immediately check myself into the hospital. I settled in, knowing I was there for 5 days and I felt safe. I knew my daughter was in good hands with his dad there. I had very structured days. We got up at 7 a.m. and had breakfast at 8 a.m. We went to group counseling twice a day and had one-on-one counseling. too. After 5 days I was ready to go home, although I don't know what I thought would change. I could go home as long as I continued to go to group counseling on an out-patient basis.

Things got worse at home. We had fights about everything. He didn't like the way I did housework or cooking or my chores. We fought about how much money I spent at the grocery store every time I went. Our worst fight was when I got a speeding ticket. He took the checkbook away and told me that if I did not have a part-time job in a week to pay for my ticket he was kicking me out. He also put me over his knee and spanked me for not minding him, an act that angers me so much on, top of everything else, that I still get mad when I think about it. I got a part-time job at a local insurance company. I got my paycheck and paid for my ticket. He had another idea: pay for room and board. So he told me if I didn't have a full-time job in two weeks he was kicking me out. Luckily, the insurance company made me an offer of a full-time job. Our fights kept getting worse, and I couldn't see a way out. If I took my son and left he would kill me. If I left without my son, I would rather die. When Matthew was two years old, Rocco told me to get dressed; he was taking me out. He drove us to a local bar. He sat me down and said, "I want you out, and I want Matthew."

"What?"

He repeated it.

I said, "No way in hell."

He grabbed me by the arm and jerked me out the door to the car. He swung open the car door and threw me in. He started hitting me in the face and head and told me to sign a paper or he would kill me right there. I had no idea what I was signing. I was bloody and hurt. I did not go to the police because I knew he would kill me, go to prison, and not bat an eye.

Two days later I packed my things and was forced to leave my baby with him. I thought I was going to die. I wanted to die. "Don't make me leave without my baby," I pleaded and pleaded. I was devastated, torn in two. I left my heart for my baby on that porch that day. It was the single most devastating experience of my life. Losing everything in a fire was nothing compared to living without my baby.

I didn't see my baby for 6 weeks, waiting on the court date. My face was puffy, and I felt weak from not eating and from crying. The judge signed the divorce decree and threw the book at me, basically. We got joint custody, but Matthew would continue to live with Rocco. I was ordered to pay $300 per month for child support on my salary of $900 per month. I was also told I had to do all the driving, which was 60 miles one way. I could see Matthew, as we both agreed, but nothing was stipulated.

I would pick him up after driving 60 miles one way on a Friday night and take him back Sunday. I cried when I picked him up, while he was with me, and had a complete breakdown every time I had to take him home. He was changing so much, and I was missing it. I wasn't tucking him in bed every night; an alcoholic was. I really didn't think I could live through this. Rocco made my life a living hell, not letting me see him some weekends just out of spite. I would drive all the way up there to pick him up, and he would throw me off his property, and I would go home without my son. I would drive home angry and defeated. He did everything he could to try to control me, using our son and my emotional unraveling and depression as a pawn like in a chess game. As my son was growing up he got grounded by Rocco for every little thing. His groundings meant that he was grounded from me. I never understood how a father could ground his child from me, the mother. We would argue on the phone. I would consult a lawyer, realize I couldn't afford it, feel defeated, and cry another week until I tried to see him again. There were times when Matthew was in grade school where I didn't see him for months.

I didn't have anyone to talk to. I didn't know any other woman who had lost her son to a horrible man and had to pay child support. I walked around in shame, shame that I didn't have my son, shame that I felt it was all my fault.

Esteem Yourself!
Take time for yourself.

Chapter 8

Ferris Wheel

In 1990, a few months after I was forced to leave, I met Monte. Rocco was still trying to control me. He demanded Monte's social security number and wanted to do a background check on him. It was a few months after the divorce, and I knew it was too soon, but I needed a distraction from missing my baby so much. Monte had the nicest smile, salt-and-pepper hair and a deep voice. He was seven years younger than me. He made me feel younger. I really liked being around him. Samantha really liked him, too.

We started dating and seeing each other a lot. He took me to the auto races, baseball games, and out to dinner. Our relationship was growing, and my daughter was getting more attached. After about a year we moved in together. Life was wonderful! He was my charm, the man of my dreams. Things were so easy and carefree. He took good care of me and did anything to make sure I didn't cry over not seeing my son. Sometimes we would go shopping, and if we could hear music on the speakers, he would grab me and would slow dance right there in the store like there was no one else around just to see me smile. We would spend our Friday nights cooking together and slow dancing or watching movies. Every Saturday morning we would go to breakfast. We would chat and sip coffee, catching up from the week.

He helped my daughter learn how to catch a softball. She loved softball and was very well known for her catching He was always very supportive of anything I wanted to do, too. He would help me with my crafts, which eventually turned into my own gift-basket business. I would make baskets; he would give me his input and even do shopping for me. He was an amazing man who I loved very dearly from the moment I met him. My daughter grew to love him, too.

My whole family liked Monte. I met his family, and we all got along so well. I didn't realize he had some deep emotional problems from abuse as a child from his father. The first sign came around the holidays. My daughter was around 13 years old, and we really took pride in putting up a nice Christmas tree with all the trimmings. We decorated it with home-made ornaments and ornaments we had made together and collected through the years.

Monte had been gone all day at his brother's house. He got home that night, and I could tell by his posture and expressions that he was angry. Almost as soon as he got in the door he looked at the tree. It was blinking different colors and had such a spirit of Christmas with all the ornaments Samantha and I had collected through the years. It was so pretty.

He picked up his bat and started swinging at the tree in anger and broke the ornaments as the tree came crashing down! My daughter went in her room and grabbed his present, which was an ashtray she had gotten him and threw it at the wall, and it broke in pieces. She was so hurt and upset. Monte and I got in a big fight, and I was yelling at him. He walked out the door. I tried to pick up the mess but I was crying so much from the hurt and disappointment I was feeling for my daughter and me. I found out later he was drunk, the first of many times I would see him that way. He was such a good man when he was sober that I forgave him.

Shortly after that, during a horrible time, to make matters worse, my daughter, who was now 14 ran away. Monte was so mean to her at this time. She kept telling me she smelled alcohol, and I didn't believe her because I didn't smell it. I didn't listen, and she got upset and went to her grandmother's, and her grandmother told the state that I disowned her, and she had nowhere to go.

By state decree I had two days to come up with $1,000. Luckily my income-tax refund came, and I was able to pay. I ended up having to pay more, too, because she ended up dropping my daughter out of school (without my consent) and putting her in a new school (without my consent, too). I went to the school and got thrown out. It was too late; they had all told her I didn't love her anymore and did not want her in my life. I tried and tried to get in touch with her, to no avail. I kept going to the school and writing letters to the state only to be ignored. One day I went to the school, and I made it as far as the cafeteria. I saw my daughter. She looked sad, like her spirit was broken. The principal saw me and threw me out! I was her mother, dammit, and I did not disown her! Give her back! She stayed with her grandmother several months. It was just long enough that Samantha finally realized she had been lied to and contacted me. I finally got her back in my home. We were very happy to be reunited.

Esteem Yourself!
Do things you are good at.

Chapter 9

Tight Rope

After five years of living together, Monte asked me to marry him. I loved Monte in a way I had not felt in a long time. However, living with him was like being in the top seat of the Ferris wheel as it stops in mid-air. That feeling of exhilaration and smelling the air while looking down on everyone. That feeling you get when you feel like you are on top of the world. Then the Ferris wheel takes motion and gains momentum and you go down to the bottom and back up again

I loved him so much that I felt I could handle anything with him. We planned a small wedding at our house, and I made the bouquets, boutonnières, and decorations myself. As soon as we were married it got worse.

It was always an emotional upheaval of some kind. We would argue about money. It was always disappearing. Through the next four years of our marriage we lost our house, had to go on food stamps, had to borrow money, separated, got back together, and he put our brand-new car in the lake.

Thinking back, it all ended just the way it started, immediately. The ending all seems kind of orchestrated as if a maestro was controlling the beat. We would be sitting on the couch all cuddled up watching television, a moment that was so perfect. Then a week or so later I would come home and find him drunk and violent.

Shortly after we got married Monte hurt his back on the job. This is when all the heavy drinking and lies started. He lied about how he hurt his back. His story kept changing.

The next few months we had back-to-back doctor appointments. We finally got the results. Monte could never work again. He would have to have surgery. There would be no income until we got a settlement. After surgery he had a long recovery. He was in pain all the time. I was exhausted being a care-giver and working full-time. The holidays were awful. I was always alone, because he would take his pain pills and pass out early. We lived on my income. I was making $36,000 as an administrator at a software company. It took two years before we received a settlement. During the two years, Monte stayed home, sank into a deep depression and started drinking heavily. He was also smoking pot to dull the pain. He was envious that I had a life at work and friends that I spent time with. He stayed in his room a lot, and I was lonely. He hated my friends.

One day we decided to go to the amusement park. He got in the wheelchair, and I wheeled him all around the amusement park. He was very angry and upset that he was in a wheelchair. He got mad at me when I hit a bump. He wouldn't even talk to me that evening. One day we went to get haircuts, and I introduced him to my stylist. She started flirting heavily with him. She ran her hands through his salt-and-pepper hair. He had thick hair, and she made a comment about how nice it was. He ended up cheating on me with her. I found they went and had coffee, and he went back to her place. She moved shortly after, and I never got to confront her. One weekend he went out of town to see his sons. I was on the computer and saw that he sent X-rated e-mails to strange women from singles sites. It was a struggle daily. I never knew what kind of trouble he would get into, especially after the surgery and all the healing time. It was especially hard on both of us. I kept noticing how much money he was spending. I found out later he was going to the casinos to pass the time away.

That October I got a phone call from my sister. Her husband had died. We packed our bags and headed to the lake for the funeral. We stayed in a log cabin on the lake not far from my sister's house. Monte was a different person. He was so loving and kind. He didn't drink at all. He was so supportive of me losing my brother-in-law. He knew how I felt about him.

When we got back we got a notice in the mail that our lawyer had a check for us. With the settlement money we got a brand new car, paid a year on a three-bedroom townhouse, and moved from our 1-bedroom apartment. We scheduled a week on a houseboat in Florida We spent our days on the boat cruising around and swimming. Our nights were spent talking, laughing, slow dancing, and going for walks. We had such an amazing time! Whenever I hear the song by Leanne Womack, "I Hope You Dance," I am taken back to that night. I was in love with the man of my dreams, and we were slow dancing on the deck of the houseboat.

When we got back in town we started moving our things into our new townhouse. We quickly got settled. I spent time unpacking, working, and shopping for things we needed. I felt like I did everything. His depression was back. He was so depressed all the time he wouldn't even leave the house to buy his own cigarettes. Being a care giver and working full-time wore on me. My mood changed. I was no longer happy. Here I was in my third marriage, and now it was falling apart due to his drinking that I could never prove he was doing. I did everything I could to make this marriage work. What else could I do? I did not want another failure/divorce on my record.

One night I caught Monte trying to hang himself. After that we were in and out of mental facilities. We went to group counseling, and he would go to AA, and I would go to Al Anon. I wrote a poem for him to read, and to this day it is framed on the wall at the AA hall.

We were driving home from a particular group session where I spoke about how Monte always took his anger out on me. He threw an ash tray at me that just missed me. He called me names, like bitch and whore. He was always yelling. He had horrible road rage. He was angry all the time.

He was particularly agitated on the way home after I mentioned all that. We got in an argument while driving, and he pinched me so hard on my thigh that I immediately bruised. Some of our other fights ended with food being thrown at me, things being knocked over, or me being shoved into the wall.

One ugly fight we had was an argument over a man I was spending time with at work. Due to not getting any attention, affection, or support at home, I was flirting with this man. One day we went and got lunch together, and he kissed me. It was a long, hard, wanting kiss. I felt guilty, so I told Monte. He blocked me in the bedroom and would not let me get out. This caused a panic in me. It ended with him throwing me out of the bedroom and forcing me to sleep on the couch.

One night, loaded on all his medicines, he fell asleep with a lit cigarette in his hand. After that I was scared to fall asleep first. This caused even more stress. I forced him to go to the doctor. He was diagnosed with borderline personality disorder, bipolar disorder, and social disorder.

He would tell me he quit drinking, but I was always afraid to go home. I would find a bottle under the cabinet and know he was drinking, but he would say, "That has been there a long time."

In my mind he seemed like some kind of magician—poof! Now you see it, now you don't. My life with him was so distorted. I lost my identity completely.

One day he picked me up from work. He was angry right from the start. I was standing on the sidewalk talking to a man on my team at work. All the way home, he accused me of cheating on him with this man. He was yelling, cussing, and driving erratically. He was driving way too fast and scaring me.

We finally got home, and he was so drunk he almost fell gathering his fishing stuff so he could leave. I felt lucky to be home. He left and squealed the tires out of the driveway. I packed my stuff and went home to Mom and Dad's. At 2 a.m. we got a phone call. Monte had been car-jacked at the lake. The new car, his billfold and wedding ring were gone. He was beat up and lying in the grass. I packed up and went back home. I felt so bad for him. It wasn't long before the real story came out. The detective contacted me to interview me. That coupled with police reports put a new light on this "crime." Monte was drunk, angry, and depressed. He purposely put the car in the lake out of anger. He took the police to the spot where he put it in at the boat ramp. The insurance didn't cover it, and the police didn't prosecute because he destroyed mutual property.

After that I no longer trusted him at all. He knew it. He started taking a major diet pill on top of all his medicines. He wasn't eating right, and he had gained fifty pounds. He couldn't work out due to the injury. He ended up being careless with the diet pills mixed with all his prescriptions and went into a coma. He was in the coma for four days. The doctor told him he was lucky to be alive. The doctors told me to keep an eye on him.

A few months later on a Friday night, I came home from work. Monte was passed out on the couch. I felt like a robot—I felt nothing. I walked into the kitchen and started fixing the spaghetti I had planned for dinner. It came to a boil at the same time I did! I was fuming. I turned off the burner. I grabbed a pitcher and filled it full of ice water. I walked over to the couch and threw the pitcher of water on him. He was wearing sweat pants and no shirt. The cold hit him fast and furious.

I said, "Good—you better wake up. I am leaving, and this is the last time you will ever lay eyes on me as your wife." By the time he was fully coherent, I slammed the door and was gone. I took an officer with me to get the rest of my stuff. Monte was sitting at the table with his gun lying there. The officer took the gun and took the bullets out. I got all my belongings I could get and left.

That Sunday, a cold January day, I made arrangements to get all the rest of my belongings. It was one of the saddest days of my life. Another failure, another loss. It was so cold outside that my tears practically froze to my face as I was taking loads out to the truck. That day I smelled the liquor on him the first time. We stood there looking around the townhouse and looking at each other, trying to figure out how we got to this horrible point where everything was over. How could it be that we had such a great marriage when he was sober and it could be ruined in a second with a bottle in his hand? How am I supposed to accept that he chose liquor over me?

That hurt so deeply. We hugged goodbye, held each other for several minutes, and cried.

The depression I felt after this third failure was insurmountable. I could barely function. I ended up in a counseling program called "Hope for Change." It was during this counseling program I found out I was "addicted to chaos." I had never even heard of this. She said I had been living such a roller coaster for so long that my mind expected it and was constantly waiting for the other shoe to drop or the rug to get pulled out from under me. I had no sense of balance in my life. It had been bad for so long I didn't even recognize the good. I went to this counseling for a year. It really helped me understand why I enabled men to hurt me and not step out of the situation. It also helped me understand why someone could choose liquor over me, which I could not come to terms with.

Esteem Yourself!

Don't do anything to undermine your level of self-esteem.

Chapter 10

The Moon Walk

For years I had nightmares of all I have been through. Every Christmas, I was haunted by that Christmas tree falling over and over. It would fall over in my mind so many times, I couldn't even focus on the holidays. To me the holidays were sad and brought on nothing but depression and despair. I realized I had to change the image in order to get over it. I started seeing the Christmas tree in a new fresh light, just like my life. My tree was standing proud, tall, and the lights were twinkling. It was no longer crashing to the ground like the way I felt when I would sink to the depths of my depression. I no longer had to fear anyone smashing my Christmas tree to the ground. I no longer had to worry about anyone hurting me. It is my choice who I let into my life. It will not be due to low self-esteem, or lack of confidence. I have felt the impact of my low self-esteem. I know what it did to me. I know what it can do to others. I can recognize it now.

When I was 42 I had a relationship with Tomas. After we had been dating for 2 years, he looked at me and said, "I want it all, the good, the bad and the ugly! Stop hiding who you are! I feel like you are hiding behind a carnival mirror, and I can't get to you because you see yourself all distorted! You don't see yourself the way I see you! You are hot!"

I remember looking at him, and I just fell into his strong arms in tears. Finally, I don't have to hide anymore. I can come out and be myself. What a shock! I am in a relationship where I am not abused, never cussed at, totally respected. Now how do I do this? Sadly it ended, but we are still friends.

As I sit here seven years later, at the age of 49, I have dated several men; none of them have been abusive. It took me a long time to learn to trust. I met Tim, whom I dated for a year, and he was my first love after Monte. He asked me to marry him, but it was way too soon, and the idea of another marriage made me cringe. I met Randy, who was sweet to me, and we dated for a short time. On the very first date he took me on a gondola ride. We sipped champagne, ate chocolates, and he handed me a rose. I never told him, but he treated me nicer than I have ever been treated. He was very charming. He showed me there are good men out there besides Tomas who will treat me right. We remain friends. I met Tony, and we dated for a while. He showed me that I can love again, and I don't have to pay an emotional price to be loved. I could call him today, and he would be there if I needed him. I met Cary, who is seven years younger, and he showed me I still have passion, and I am still a desirable woman at my age. I have many men friends I can call if I need something.

I realize that I don't have everything I want. Having been in bad relationships and the guilt I felt has kept my life on hold for way longer than I ever dreamed. But I don't hate my life. I can't be anyone else. I can only be me. I am a complete, 100% whole woman. I am no longer in pieces. I remember what my mom told me at the age of 12, and how I see it more clearly now. Time has gone by, but I have healed, I have forgiven, and I can move on to a good, healthy relationship. I have overcome great obstacles. I do want to get out of bed now. I do have a reason to live. I can recognize a good man now. I can now recognize good character traits. They are important to me. For a while I didn't know who I was and didn't have anything to give. I no longer feel shame for choosing three wrong men back to back who were mentally, physically, and emotionally abusive. I am no longer the victim of these men. Yes, there was loss, but through that loss became a tremendous strength that made me who I am today. I am stronger than I have ever been. No man will ever lay a hand on me. I will never again enable a man to drink heavily or do drugs in my presence.

If I could change one thing, I would not have my precious kids from two different fathers. But if I had changed one thing I would not be this strong, beautiful woman with high self-esteem, confidence, able to function, think clearly, and learn new things. I would not have achieved a college degree and made it through the darkest side of depression and come through on the other side with flying colors. I like my life. I enjoy the small things now. I don't wake up with the heaviness of my past on my heart.

I found out that Jared's wife of 22 years, Ciera, left him for a younger man. I wonder how many years of abuse she had to put up with. She had three daughters, she got the BMW, and when she got the $300,000 house she left him and it behind. He called to tell me the news, and he said he told his daughters we were getting back together.

"What? You think I waited all these years for you? Are you crazy? You got just what you deserved, Jared!" That felt so good!

Rocco still drinks and has no relationship with his son, Matthew, at all. Matthew and I are as close as a mother and son can be. I see him all the time. I thank God for that every day.

I saw Monte the other day. We hugged and got caught up on each other's lives. He still says he is sorry, and he still wants me back in his life. He says losing me was the biggest mistake he ever made. It makes me sad, but I could never go back to someone who could choose a bottle of liquor over me. It has been 7 years, and I am a completely different woman.

The wounds I suffered from the abuse from these 3 men, I look at differently now. Instead of feeling like a victim, I feel strong and able to tackle anything. When I was a wife, I was the best one I could be. Silly to think about now, but I can remember when I made eggs or toast, I always made sure my husband got the good eggs and the non-burnt toast. I got the over-scrambled eggs and burnt toast. Now I feel like I deserve the good eggs and the non-burnt toast. I realize now the behavior traits I had as a woman with low self esteem. I always made the small things seem insurmountable, I never trusted my own opinion about anything. I withdrew from everyone socially. I also accentuated the negative, never seeing the positive. I felt I didn't deserve anything special. For almost 3 decades, I lost my identity. I was a wife to men who did not know what the word meant.

I gave up my own opinions and beliefs for the sake of men in my life. I gave up my social life, I withdrew from my friends, and didn't try anything new. I now put myself first. I think about what I want out of life. It is my life, and I decide who comes in and who goes out. I feel worthy of someone great.

The other day I went to a carnival in town. I took my 9-year-old grandson and my 18-year-old son. We had a lot of fun that day. We ate cotton candy and played ring toss. We walked up on the carnival mirrors. I took a good, long look in the mirrors. I saw myself clearly and not distorted.

I saw a 49-year-old woman, with a little gray in her brown hair, a few pounds overweight, who has let go of the hardships of the past, embraced the present, and is looking forward to the future.

I didn't focus on the distorted images…. I walked away and chose me, and I am enough.

A Carnival Mirror hides as much as it reveals.

LOW SELF-ESTEEM

How Can We Stop the Cycle of Children/ Teens Being Raised with Low Self-esteem?

Build a positive self image right from the start. Be generous and praise them often. When you feel good about something your children have done—tell them. Words of encouragement will go a long way towards building self-esteem. As a parent, we are quick to express negative feelings to children when they do something wrong, but we forget to say positive things.

Teach your child to practice positive "self-talk." Self-talk is important in everything we do. Depression and anxiety is often a smokescreen caused by negative self-talk. What we think determines how we feel, and how we feel determines our behavior. So if your children say, "It is my fault we lost the game today," have them change it to, "It is okay if the team lost today. I tried my best." This way your children's negative self-talk has just been changed to positive self-talk. Help your children develop positive character traits. If they are kind, tell them that. Help your children learn to focus on their strengths by pointing them out to them. Help them to learn to have a good sense of humor and that sometimes you can laugh at yourself. Teach your children about decision-making and to recognize when they have made a good decision. Encourage them to develop hobbies and interests that they will enjoy. Teach your children how to make lots of friends and feel comfortable making them. Help your children learn to handle anger in a positive way. When my daughter was younger and playing video games, the minute she showed frustration in a bad way, she lost the game for an hour or so. She remembers this and does the same thing with her 9-year-old son.

If your children have something important coming up and they are scared they can't do it, sit down with them and talk to them about why they are afraid. I use the following exercise on my kids:

Draw a line on a piece of paper and number it in 20s to 100; 100 is the worst scenario. Let's use the example that my daughter is going on a job interview. What is the absolute worst thing that can happen? Her answer, "I will make a fool of myself."

So you mark that at the 100 mark. Then what is the next worst thing that can happen? "They won't like me."

So you would mark that at the 80 mark. So you see by the time they break it down and you get to 20 or 0 they have voiced all their fears and have seen them on a scale. This helps to relieve the anxiety they feel.

How can parents spot low self-esteem in their children?

Quitting: If children are unable to succeed at a particular task, they will get frustrated and quit.

Avoiding: They will avoid going out for a play, or a team, because they are so sure they will fail.

Controlling: They attempt to take command and become dictatorial, telling others what to do.

Bullying: If they are feeling inadequate they might resort to aggressive behavior.

Use these tips if you suffer from low self-esteem.

Esteem Yourself!

Set goals. Even small ones. This will build your confidence and your self-esteem.

If you have the blues, recognize it. Take control of bad feelings.

Think positive.

Repeat a "mantra" every day. "Today, I am a confident person."

Take on something new.

Laugh daily.

Acknowledge your strengths and weaknesses. You are valuable no matter what they are. Work on your weaknesses.

What do people notice about you? It is something negative, work on it.

When someone compliments you acknowledge it by saying, "Thank you." It is your compliment. Take it.

You can only change you.

Spend time with positive people.

Don't put up with anyone being mean to you or putting you down.

If anyone ever lays a hand on you—walk away at that moment. Know that it will not get better. It will get worse, and you do not deserve to be hit.

Don't compare yourself to anyone else. Compare yourself to yourself daily. Strive to make improvements.

Take time for yourself.

Be present. Be in the moment. Don't worry about tomorrow.

Know that your level of self-esteem affects your life in all areas.

Low self-esteem can cause bad choices.

Don't do anything to undermine your level of self-esteem.

Reward yourself for small successes.

Take responsibility for yourself, your choices, and your actions.

Be your own best friend.

Decorate your own soul.

Self-esteem Tips for Teens

Teen Esteem!

Do not compare yourself to others.

Puberty is different for everyone.

Do not give in to the peer pressure.

Have a "go-to" person, someone you can talk to about you.

Rise above any negative comments.

Care more about how you see yourself than how others see you.

Celebrate a good body image.

Be happy the way you are.

Enjoy spending time with you.

Laugh often.

Keep an "Esteem-Journal;" write down all good things you do and the compliments you get.

Celebrate small successes.

Be the best you can be.

Make your own decisions.

Acknowledge your personal worth.

You are enough! Period.

Watch out for situational attacks on your esteem. Don't acknowledge it, and walk away.

Have a one-night-stand with yourself. Stay in and read, do research on something you are curious about, do a craft, watch your favorite move, give yourself a facial, condition your hair.

You are worthy to be loved, cared for, nurtured, supported, listened to, recognized, and encouraged.

If anyone lays a hand on you, walk away.

Be aware of your strengths and abilities.

Be aware of areas that need work, and grow in those areas.

Esteem yourself daily.

Destroy your mental tape if it has anything negative about you. Replace with positive self-talk.

Do not change to please other people.

Be strong and say NO!

Bored? What would do if you were 5?

Be true to yourself.

If you did fail at something, focus on what you learned from the failure and not the failure itself.

Let's Look at the Difference Between

Healthy Self-esteem and Low Self-esteem

As children, we believe what we are told about ourselves. If you call children "losers" or "failures" they will think the same thing as adults. The message will be loud and clear. Children told they are "stupid" will live with these messages and the negative self-talk will keep them from trying new things. They will hold back due to the fear of feeling "stupid."

Negative "self-talk" is usually a mixture of poor logic, half-truths and distortions of reality. For some people it has become a daily inner dialogue that causes negative emotions, such as pessimism, fear, anxiety, as well as self-sabotaging behaviors.

Children or teens with high self-esteem will be able to:

handle frustration
assume responsibility
handle both positive and negative emotions
take pride in their accomplishments
act independently

Children with low self-esteem will:

put themselves down
feel unwanted or unloved

not be able to tolerate normal levels of frustration

be influenced easily

avoid trying new things

Mental Aerobics

I had listened to negative "self-talk" most of my life, and I had to learn how to break free from that. I learned the following exercises to help fight it. Rocco told me that no other man would ever want me. I had that negative "self-talk" for years. Finally, I stepped up and said, "Who is he to tell me that? I know what I have to offer." Below are my mental aerobics I use to take a step out of the negative self-talk:

Instead of saying "I am such an idiot" change that to "I will do better next time."

Catch yourself and recognize the negative self-talk and stop it immediately.

It is okay to be less than perfect.

Be proud of what you have done and what you are working on.

If you have negative people in your life, learn not to listen to them.

You can't change your past, but you can change the way you talk to yourself.

Say, "Today I am going to be the best I can be."

Do not be critical of your body or your mind.

Do not speak negatively about anyone else.

Instead of saying, "I can't do this," say, "I am willing to try and do the best I can."

An Exercise to See How Low Self-esteem Affects Us

Find a long feather. Put it in the middle of a shadow box. Every day when you hear negative self-talk look at the feather. Imagine tearing out one of the feather's branches for every negative thing you say to yourself. It won't be long until you run out of feathers and your stem is bare. Think about what that does to your spirit.

Instead, look at the feather and see how pretty it is, and notice the colors and the texture. Think about all the positive things you have done, and keep your feather intact.

Dating/Relationships and Low Self-esteem

I entered the online dating world at a time when I was at my lowest. I dated some men who I wouldn't even think about looking at now. I dated what I now call "bottom feeders." These are men who look for women at their lowest so they can take advantage of them. With my low self esteem, I had the tendency to seek out men that exploited my weaknesses. I did not believe in my own self-worth, so trying to attract a loving partner when suffering from low self esteem was an uphill battle.

Finding love in all the wrong places is a bad side effect of low self esteem. You attract to you what you believe about yourself. Now that I have improved my self esteem I am attracting men who do not have low self esteem, have good character, and know their worth. I learned that positive self-esteem needs to be deep-rooted before you engage in any serious dating relationship.

If you are dating with low self esteem, one of two things is likely to happen: you will have difficulty attracting a partner because you are projecting insecurity and neediness, or you may attract a partner who is less than ideal for you. You may end up being treated abusively physically, mentally, or both, because deep down you don't believe you deserve better.

Low self-esteem dating is a way to fill a void. You're likely to feel especially vulnerable after a divorce or any relationship that ended in disappointment. Rejection is very damaging to your self-esteem, and you may feel like you have to prove to yourself and others that you are still loveable. You rush in headfirst with the first man you date, only to be disappointed again. The more disappointment you experience, the more you come to expect to be.

Do not date anyone you don't feel good about. When the date is over ask yourself these questions:

"How does he make me feel?"
"What do I get out of this relationship?"
"Is this man good enough for my standards?"

Begin working on your self-respect and improving your self esteem. Look for your good qualities and build on them. As your self esteem starts to improve start going on some dates, but take it slowly. Going on one or two dates with someone doesn't mean you have to rush into a relationship. Each person you date is not going to be the last potential partner you ever come across. Take your time to learn about their character.

When you can honestly say you love and respect yourself, you will be in a much better position to find an appropriate partner and to recognize when someone doesn't really have much to offer. You'll be able to take your time, and keep things in perspective. You won't rush into something you'll regret. Take the time to become the person you would fall in love with in order to attract the same caliber of man to you. Make sure you are happy with who you are first and foremost. When you feel like you don't even need a man, that is when you are healthy enough to have an excellent relationship!

One thing I have learned is to stop giving 100% of myself to anyone. I hold back 20%. This 20% keeps me grounded, and I don't lose my heart. This way if a man leaves me or I see his true colors later on, I will be disappointed but not devastated. I will know I can move on with less heartbreak.

Self-esteem is the heart of our personality. Once you have a healthy self esteem, don't let anyone chip away at it. It is yours to keep. You decide who you let in your life. You have choices. You will realize its strength in your life as you make better decisions for yourself.

Self-esteem comes from finding the goodness—the truth—the essence—of you within you, bringing it to the surface, learning to recognize it and handle life's challenges from a place of strength.

YOU ARE ENOUGH.

A carnival mirror is like being unmasked at the Mardi Gras.
You no longer have anything to hide behind.

CPSIA information can be obtained at www.ICGtesting.com
Printed in the USA
BVOW02s1050040215

386355BV00001B/68/P